D1271826

LEARNING ABOUT DOGS
THE DACHSHUND

BY CHARLOTTE WILCOX

Consultant:
Ann Gordon
Board of Directors
Dachshund Club of America
AKC Dachshund Judge

CANCEl

CAPSTONE
HIGH-INTEREST
BOOKS

an imprint of Capstone Press
Mankato, Minnesota

Capstone High-Interest Books are published by Capstone Press
151 Good Counsel Drive, P.O. Box 669, Mankato, Minnesota 56002
http://www.capstone-press.com

Library of Congress Cataloging-in-Publication Data

Wilcox, Charlotte.
The dachshund/by Charlotte Wilcox.
    p.cm.—(Learning about dogs)
    Includes bibliographical references (p. 45) and index.
    ISBN 0-7368-0763-2
    1. Dachshunds—Juvenile literature. [1.Dachshunds. 2. Dogs. 3. Pets]
I. Title. II. Series
SF429.D25 W53 2001
636.753'8—dc21   00-009810

Summary: Discusses the history, development, habits, uses, and care of Dachshunds.

Editorial Credits
Leah K. Pockrandt, editor; Lois Wallentine, product planning editor; Timothy Halldin,
    cover designer and illustrator; Katy Kudela, photo researcher

Photo Credits
Cheryl A. Ertelt, 21, 28, 34
Jean M. Fogle, 9
Kent and Donna Dannen, 10, 12, 16, 27, 33, 38, 40–41
Mark Raycroft, cover, 1, 4, 6, 18, 22, 24, 30
Norvia Behling, 37
Rachel Hoffman, 15

1 2 3 4 5 6 06 05 04 03 02 01

c.1

TABLE OF CONTENTS

Quick Facts about the Dachshund

Description

Height: Dachshunds stand 5 to 9 inches
(13 to 23 centimeters) tall. Height is
measured from the ground to the withers.
The withers are the tops of the shoulders.

Weight: Most Dachshunds weigh between
5 and 32 pounds (2.3 and 15 kilograms).

**Physical
features:** Dachshunds have very short legs, long
bodies, and long ears. Dachshunds can
be either miniature or standard. Miniature

Dachshunds are smaller than standard Dachshunds. Dachshunds' coats can be short and smooth, rough and wiry, or long and silky.

Color: One-colored Dachshunds are red-brown or cream. Two-colored Dachshunds' coats can be black or several shades of brown or gray with tan markings. Dachshunds also may have a pattern of light and dark spots called dapple. Other Dachshunds may have a striped pattern called brindle.

Development

Place of origin: Dachshunds came from Germany.

History of breed: The Dachshunds' history is unclear. They may descend from ancient dogs of Egypt or Europe.

Numbers: In 1999, the American Kennel Club registered 50,772 Dachshunds. In 1999, the Canadian Kennel Club registered 1,311 Dachshunds. Owners who register their Dachshunds record their dogs' breeding records with an official club.

Uses: Most Dachshunds in North America are family pets. Some Dachshunds are used for hunting. Some are used for search-and-rescue work.

CHAPTER 1

THE BADGER DOG

Most people recognize a Dachshund (DAHKS-hunt) by its short legs. The Dachshund has a long, low body. This body shape has earned it nicknames such as "wiener dog" and "sausage dog."

Dachshunds were bred in Germany to hunt badgers, foxes, and hares. These animals live in burrows underground. Dachshunds were trained to dig into the animals' holes and pull the animals out. The German word for badger is "dachs." The word for dog is "hund." Together, Dachshund means "badger dog" in German.

People may recognize Dachshunds by their body shape.

Hunting Qualities

Dogs that hunt below ground are called terriers or "earth dogs." Dachshunds have many terrier qualities. They have strong shoulders and front legs for digging. They can easily crawl into tight spaces. Like terriers, Dachshunds do not seem to be afraid of larger animals.

Dogs that hunt by scent are called hounds. Dachshunds share some qualities with hounds. They have a very sensitive sense of smell. They also have long, droopy ears and a loud bark.

Some people think the Dachshund's short legs are a problem. But Dachshunds have short legs for a good reason. They were bred to tunnel into burrows after wild animals. Shorter legs allow Dachshunds to crawl into smaller holes. Being short also helps them go through brush and thickets.

Dachshunds have other qualities for underground hunting. Their legs are closer

Dachshunds use their paws to dig into burrows when they hunt.

to their bodies than the legs of most other breeds. This helps them fit better into tight places. Their legs can move without being squeezed too much. People can see a Dachshund's long tail even when the rest of the body is down in a hole.

Miniature and standard Dachshunds can have one of three different coat types.

Dachshunds use their physical qualities when they hunt. Dachshunds have extra-strong jaws that they use to bite and hold onto animals that they catch. Their long ears may help direct scents into their noses.

Different Types of Dachshunds

Dachshunds can be one of two sizes. These sizes are miniature and standard. Adult miniature Dachshunds weigh 11 pounds (5 kilograms) or less. Adult standard Dachshunds weigh more than 11 pounds. Dogs are considered adults when they are 1 year old.

Dachshunds may have one of three coat types. These types are smooth, wirehaired, and longhaired. Smooth Dachshunds usually are called "smooths." Breeders prefer to keep coat types separate. They usually do not breed Dachshunds of one coat type with another type.

Each of the three coat types can be either miniature or standard size. This makes a total of six different types of Dachshunds.

CHAPTER 2

THE BEGINNINGS OF THE BREED

The Dachshund name is German in origin. But in Germany, a Dachshund is often called a teckel (TEK-uhl). Some people think the name teckel is Egyptian. Others believe the name is another form of dachel (DAHK-uhl). This German word is a shortened form of Dachshund.

Dachshunds may have originated in ancient Egypt. A long-bodied, short-legged dog appears in an ancient Egyptian drawing. Ancient statues of long-bodied, short-legged dogs also have been found in South America and China.

Short-legged dogs have existed in Europe for about 500 years. Pictures and writings tell of badger dogs in the 1500s and 1600s. In some ways, these dogs looked like modern Dachshunds. They had hound qualities such as long ears, big heads, and crooked front legs.

Dachshunds also are called teckels and dachels.

Centuries ago, forests covered much of Europe. People cleared forestland for farms and towns during the 1700s and 1800s. Some of the forest animals caused problems for farmers and townspeople. These animals included bears, wild boars, badgers, foxes, and hares. The people used many types of dogs to help to get rid of these game animals.

Hunting Forest Animals

People used large, powerful dogs to hunt large animals such as bears and wild boars. But big dogs could not catch small game if the hunted animals escaped down their burrows. Even smaller hounds had a difficult time. Their legs were too long to crawl into the holes. Dogs with short legs such as Dachshunds are best for catching animals in their burrows.

Dachshunds must be brave. They must be willing to fight fierce animals such as badgers if needed. Dachshunds also do not seem to be afraid when they dive into dark tunnels.

Badgers protect themselves in many ways. Badgers fight fiercely if they are cornered. They may attack a dog or person if there is no way to

Early breeders wanted Dachshunds with the shortest legs.

escape. They also can dig very fast. A badger can dig a new burrow in seconds.

Selective Breeding

Dachshunds' short legs are the result of selective breeding. Early Dachshund breeders carefully chose dogs with the qualities that they wanted. They matched male and female dogs with the shortest legs that they could find. They expected most of the puppies to have short legs.

Breeders used selective breeding to produce the kind of Dachshunds they wanted.

After the puppies grew up, those with longer legs were not bred. Over many years, breeders chose parents with shorter and shorter legs. They also chose dogs that were strong and would chase game without showing fear. After several generations, breeders knew that most Dachshund puppies would have these traits.

Changing the Badger Dog

Breeders crossed various terriers and hounds to produce the type of dog that they wanted. They used selective breeding to produce strong dogs with short legs. In France, these dogs were called Bassets. This word means "low-set" in French. In Germany, these dogs were called Dachshunds. At first, the two breeds were similar.

Over time, the German breeders changed their badger dog. They no longer bred dogs with crooked legs and loose skin. They bred dogs with shorter, straighter legs. They bred for narrower bodies, smaller heads, and tighter skin.

Dachshunds kept some of the hound qualities they shared with Bassets. They kept the hound's keen sense of smell and scent-tracking ability. Dachshunds also kept the loud bark.

By the late 1800s, Dachshunds were popular hunting dogs in Europe. Queen Victoria of England received a pet Dachshund in 1839. The next year, she married Prince Albert of Germany. He moved to England and brought more Dachshunds with him. Dachshunds were soon as popular as pets and hunting dogs in England as they were in Germany.

CHAPTER 3

THE DEVELOPMENT OF THE BREED

In 1840, German dog breeders published their first book of pedigrees. A pedigree is similar to a family tree. A book of pedigrees shows the parents, grandparents, and earlier ancestors of specific dogs. The first book included 54 Dachshunds. Later books included Dachshund family trees starting in 1859. The pedigrees of many current Dachshunds go back to these books.

Dog breeding was a popular hobby during the late 1800s. Dog clubs started to register purebred dogs. People also started to show dogs. In 1866, a Dachshund first appeared at an English dog show. Dachshunds became a separate breed class in English shows in 1873.

At that time, German breeders produced most of the Dachshunds still. In 1879, some German

English Dachshund owners used the German breed standard to write an English breed standard.

Dachshund breeders wrote a breed standard of what the ideal Dachshund should look like. In 1881, English owners used this standard to start the English Dachshund Club. This was the first Dachshund club in the world. The German Dachshund Club began in 1888.

Changing the Dachshund's Coat

At first, all standard Dachshunds had a smooth coat. They hunted game such as fox and badger. Some people used them to hunt larger game such as deer or wild boar.

Dachshunds were not large enough to catch or kill large game. But Dachshunds were good at tracking animals after hunters wounded them. They could run through thick brush because they were short. Taller dogs sometimes got tangled in brush.

Breeders used selective breeding to create Dachshunds with thicker coats. Tracking game through brush and thickets was hard on a dog's coat. The Dachshund's soft, smooth coat provided little protection. The dog's skin was easily scratched and cut.

Longhaired coats better protect dachshunds from the heat and cold.

Some breeders decided that longer hair might better protect the dogs against brush and thickets. They also thought longer hair might keep the dogs warm and dry. It is not really known how breeders produced dogs with longer hair. Some people believe that the long coat was a result of breeding Dachshunds with spaniels. Others believe that the long coat was the product of selective Dachshund breeding. Some smooth Dachshunds had longer hair than other Dachshunds. Breeders then bred

Wirehaired coats gave dachshunds more protection while running through thick brush.

dogs with longer hair to each other. They continued this process until the coat became longer and longer.

Later, some breeders decided that Dachshunds needed even more protection when the dogs were hunting. These dogs hunted through a variety of plants and trees that could injure them. The breeders decided that a short, wiry coat would give the dogs a great deal of protection. They crossbred their Dachshunds with wirehaired terrier breeds. They then used selective breeding with their Dachshunds. This process resulted in Dachshunds with thicker, coarser coats. The wirehaired coat protected Dachshunds better when running through thick brush.

Breeding for Smaller Size

Standard Dachshunds were a good size for hunting. They were small enough to chase badgers down burrows. They were large enough to track wild boars. They were strong enough to fight either animal if necessary. But they were still too large to fit inside small hare burrows.

Breeders wanted an even smaller Dachshund. They used selective breeding to create the miniature Dachshund. Miniature Dachshunds could easily hunt small animals such as hares.

Selective breeding kept the Dachshund qualities in the smaller dog. Miniature Dachshunds have the same coat types as standard Dachshunds.

CHAPTER 4

THE DACHSHUND TODAY

Dachshunds arrived in North America around 1875. Owners first used them to catch rabbits and rats. Today, the Dachshund is one of the most popular pet breeds in the United States.

Dog clubs approve the breed standard for various breeds. The breed standard includes a breed's ideal height, weight, colors, and other features. It explains the appearance of the breed. Judges use the breed standard to judge dogs in dog shows. The American Kennel Club (AKC) registered 50,772 Dachshunds in 1999. The Canadian Kennel Club (CKC) registered 1,311 Dachshunds in 1999.

Dachshunds have many recognizable qualities. Their short legs and long bodies make them easy to identify. Dachshunds also have a large chest and

Dachshunds' recognizable qualities are included in the breed standard.

a well-muscled body. They have long noses and ears. They often hold their tails straight out behind them as they walk.

Standard and miniature Dachshunds look the same except for their size. Miniature Dachshunds cannot weigh more than 11 pounds (5 kilograms) after they are 1 year old. Some weigh as little as 5 pounds (2.3 kilograms). Dachshunds that weigh more than 11 pounds are considered standard Dachshunds. Most standard Dachshunds weigh more than 16 pounds (7.3 kilograms). Some weigh as much as 32 pounds (15 kilograms).

Dachshunds' height varies. The shortest miniatures are about 5 inches (13 centimeters) tall. The tallest standards are about 9 inches (23 centimeters) tall. Height is measured from the ground to the withers. The withers are the top of the shoulders.

Coat Types

Dachshunds can have a variety of coats. These coat types are smooth, wirehaired, and longhaired. Smooth Dachshunds are the most common. Their short, shiny coats are silky and soft. They also have long, pointed tails.

Wheatens are light-colored wirehaired Dachshunds.

Wirehaired Dachshunds have thick, coarse coats. The rough fur is short over most of the body. Wirehaired Dachshunds have furry beards, eyebrows, and ears.

Longhaired Dachshunds have long, silky hair. The hair sometimes is a bit wavy. The hair is longer on the lower part of the body and the tail.

Dachshund Colors

Dachshunds can be a variety of colors and patterns. The most common color for one-colored

One of the Dachshund patterns is dapple.

Dachshunds is red. Smooth Dachshunds often are red. Red usually is deep red-brown. But the color also can be lighter. Some red Dachshunds have a mixture of black and red hairs.

One-colored Dachshunds also can be cream. This color ranges from pale yellow to beige. Light-colored wirehaired Dachshunds are called wheatens. More wirehaired Dachshunds are light-colored than longhaired or smooth Dachshunds. This especially is true in the miniature variety.

Two-colored Dachshunds have tan markings on another basic color. The basic color may be black, chocolate, or one of several types of gray. Gray sometimes is called blue. It ranges from very light to dark. Fawn is a light brown-gray color. Fawn also is called Isabella.

The tan markings of the basic color are found on specific parts of the body. They are most noticeable on the head, feet, and chest.

Wild boar consists of a basic color with tan markings. The basic color is a mixture of black, brown, and gray hairs. Wild boar with tan is a common coloring for wirehaired Dachshunds.

Dachshunds may have patterns called dapple or brindle. Any Dachshund color can have these patterns. Single dapples have lighter and darker spots of the same color. Double dapples have white spots along with the lighter and darker colored spots. Brindle is a pattern of dark stripes over another color. A piebald is a primarily white Dachshund with a pattern of large, dark-colored spots on its body. This pattern is not mentioned in the breed standards and is uncommon. But piebalds have been shown at dog shows.

CHAPTER 5

OWNING A DACHSHUND

Dachshunds are one of North America's most popular dogs. Most people find Dachshunds through clubs. Dachshund clubs help people find good breeders who raise quality dogs. Some people get Dachshunds from rescue shelters. Rescue shelters offer dogs for adoption. Dachshund clubs throughout North America offer rescue services for Dachshunds that need homes.

Dachshund Trials

Many owners enjoy attending trials with their Dachshunds. Dogs win ribbons at these events hosted by dog clubs. Trials are important for breeds that now are mainly pets. Modern Dachshunds seldom use their hunting skills.

People get Dachshunds from a variety of sources.

At trials, Dachshunds can use the skills that were bred into the breed.

At field trials, Dachshunds track live rabbits in a fenced field. Dogs are judged on how well they follow the rabbit's scent. At den trials, dogs run a challenging course that includes an underground tunnel. The tunnel is only 9 inches (23 centimeters) high. A cage of rats is at the far end of the tunnel. Dogs are judged on how fast they run the course and find the rats. The dogs do not catch or kill the animals that they are finding.

Caring for a Dachshund

Dachshunds make good pets. But they are not well suited to living outside. Dachshunds should live in a house with people. They make good housedogs because they are cleaner than most other dog breeds. Dachshunds often lick themselves clean similar to the way cats do. Dachshunds also do not have a strong odor that can be a problem with other breeds.

Smooth Dachshunds do not need much grooming. But their coats may not be warm enough in cold weather. Some owners put sweaters on their smooth Dachshunds during

At field trials, a Dachshund is judged on how well it tracks the rabbit.

cold weather. Wirehaired and longhaired Dachshunds need more grooming than smooth Dachshunds do. Owners should brush their dogs' coats to remove tangles.

Dachshund owners also need to groom their dogs in other ways. Dachshunds need their ears cleaned and checked often for disease. They also need their teeth cleaned regularly. Owners should use special dog toothpaste. Dogs cannot

Owners need to control the amount of food their Dachshunds eat.

use toothpaste made for people because it must be spit out. They need toothpaste that they can swallow. Dogs cannot spit.

Dachshunds also need plenty of exercise to keep them active and healthy. Owners may walk their dogs or play games with them. Dachshunds seem to enjoy chasing balls or other toys.

Most Dachshunds are healthy and live long lives. But some Dachshunds have back problems. Dachshunds who jump on and off furniture or walk up and down long, steep stairs may strain their backs. This strain may result in injuries. Owners need to watch for signs of back pain in their Dachshunds. Owners should take these dogs to a veterinarian. Veterinarians can treat many back problems successfully.

Feeding a Dachshund

The best diet for Dachshunds is dog food. Pet stores sell several forms of dog food. The most common forms are dry kibble, semi-moist food, and canned food. Dachshunds can eat any of these forms.

Dachshunds should not gain too much weight. Overweight Dachshunds are not healthy. Adult Dachshunds should eat low-fat dog food. They should eat about 1 cup of food each day per 15 pounds (6.8 kilograms) of body weight. Most owners divide the food into two meals.

Some foods are dangerous for dogs. Chocolate can be poisonous for some dogs. Dogs also can get sick from spicy or fatty foods. Small or sharp bones are not good for dogs. They can injure dogs' throats and stomachs. Fish and chicken bones especially are unsafe for dogs.

All dogs need plenty of fresh, clean water. They should have water available at all times. Dogs need to be able to drink when they are thirsty.

Medical Care

Dachshunds need an annual checkup to prevent diseases. At this medical exam, the veterinarian may give vaccinations to the dog. Dogs need these shots of medicine every year to protect them from illness and disease. The veterinarian also may take blood samples to check whether the dog has certain diseases.

Veterinarians also check dogs for parasites such as heartworms, fleas, ticks, and mites. Owners can give their Dachshunds pills to protect them from heartworms. Mosquitoes carry these tiny worms. They enter a dog's heart and slowly destroy it. Dogs also need a yearly checkup for other types of worms.

Owners must check their Dachshunds for ticks often during warm weather. Some ticks carry Lyme disease. This illness can disable or

Dachshunds should not gain too much weight.

kill an animal or person. Fleas, lice, and mites are tiny insects that live on a dog's skin. Owners may use flea collars or apply medicine to their dogs to keep these insects away. Owners should use caution and consult a veterinarian before using these products.

Dachshunds need time outside.

Living with a Dachshund

Dachshunds are loving pets. Most Dachshunds behave well with children. Dachshunds usually enjoy people.

Dachshunds need time to play outside. Owners should keep them in a fenced yard or on a leash when outside. Dachshunds were bred to dig. Owners must be careful so their dogs do not dig under fences and get out.

Owners should mark their dogs to identify them if the dogs become lost. Some owners have their telephone number on their dog's collar or tags. Some get their dog tattooed with a patterned mark in the skin. The tattoo is made of tiny ink drops. The tattoo contains an identification number that will help locate a dog's owner. It is usually placed on the inside of a hind leg.

The microchip is another way to identify dogs. This tiny computer chip is about the size of a grain of rice. A veterinarian surgically inserts the microchip under a dog's skin. It is usually located under the skin on the back of the neck. A veterinarian or shelter worker can scan the microchip if a lost dog is found. The microchip contains the owner's name, address, and telephone number. The microchip also may contain the dog's AKC or CKC registration number.

Today, few Dachshunds are used to hunt. People enjoy them for many reasons. Dachshunds are unusual looking yet handsome. Many people appreciate the breed's unusual looks, intelligence, and curious, lively nature.

Hindquarters

Tail

Hock

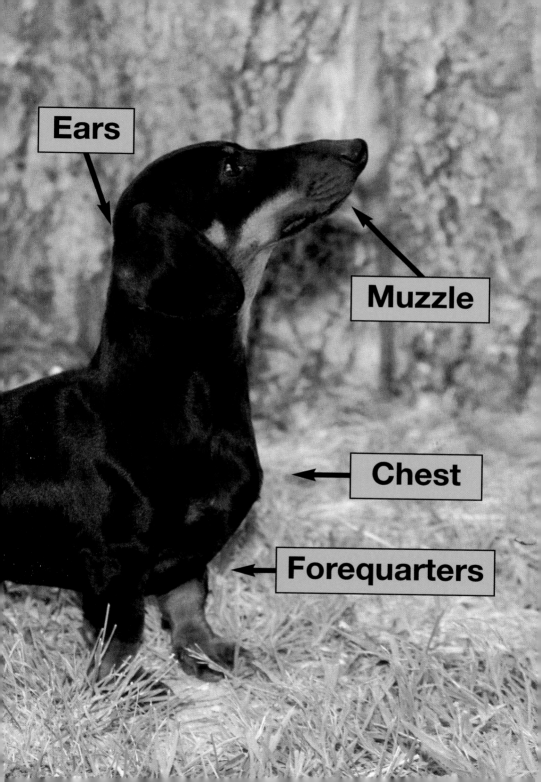

Ears

Muzzle

Chest

Forequarters

Quick Facts about Dogs

A male dog is called a dog. A female dog is called a bitch. A newborn puppy is called a whelp until it no longer needs its mother's milk. A young dog is called a puppy until it is 1 year old. A family of puppies born at one time is called a litter.

Origin: All dogs, wolves, coyotes, and dingoes descended from a single wolf-like species. People have trained dogs throughout history.

Types: About 350 official dog breeds exist in the world. Dogs can be different sizes and colors. Adult dogs weigh between 2 pounds (.9 kilogram) to more than 200 pounds (91 kilograms). They range from 5 inches (13 centimeters) to 36 inches (91 centimeters) tall.

Reproduction: Most dogs mature between 6 and 18 months. Puppies are born two months after breeding. A female can have two litters per year. An average litter is three to six puppies. Litters of 15 or more puppies are possible.

Development: Whelps are born with their eyes and ears closed. Their eyes and ears open one to two weeks after birth. Whelps try to walk when they are about 2 weeks old. Their teeth begin to come in when they are about 3 weeks old.

Life span: Most dogs are fully grown at 2 years old. With good care, many dogs can live 10 years or longer.

Smell: Dogs have a strong sense of smell. It is many times stronger than a person's sense of smell. Most dogs use their noses more than their eyes and ears. They recognize people, animals, and objects just by smelling them. They may recognize smells from long distances. They also may remember smells for long periods of time.

Hearing: Dogs hear better than people do. Dogs can hear noises from long distances. They also can hear high-pitched sounds that people cannot hear.

Sight: Dogs' eyes are farther to the sides of their heads than people's eyes are. They can see twice as wide around their heads as people can. Most scientists believe that dogs can see some colors.

Touch: Dogs seem to enjoy being petted more than almost any other animal. They also can feel vibrations from approaching trains or the beginnings of earthquakes or storms.

Taste: Dogs do not have a strong sense of taste. This is partly because their sense of smell is stronger than their sense of taste. This also is partly because dogs swallow food too quickly to taste it well. Dogs prefer certain types of foods. This may be because they like the smell of certain foods better than the smell of other foods.

Navigation: Dogs often can find their way through crowded streets or across miles of wilderness without guidance. This is a special ability that scientists do not fully understand.

Words to Know

breed standard (BREED STAN-durd)—a written description of what an ideal dog of a certain breed should look like

burrow (BUR-oh)—a tunnel or hole in the ground made or used by an animal

pedigree (PED-uh-gree)—a list of an animal's ancestors

selective breeding (si-LEK-tiv BREED-ing)—the practice of carefully choosing animals to mate with each other in order to get certain qualities in their young

tattoo (ta-TOO)—a word or picture printed onto an animal's skin with ink and needles; owners may have an identification number tattooed on their dogs.

veterinarian (vet-ur-uh-NER-ee-uhn)—a doctor who is trained to diagnose and treat sick or injured animals

withers (WITH-urz)—the tops of a dog's shoulders

To Learn More

American Kennel Club. *The Complete Dog Book for Kids.* New York: Howell Book House, 1996.

Gordon, Ann. *The Dachshund: A Dog for Town and Country.* Howell Best of Breed. New York: Howell Book House, 2000.

Kallen, Stuart A. *Dachshunds.* Dogs. Edina, Minn.: Abdo & Daughters Publishing, 1998.

Quasha, Jennifer. *The Story of the Dachshund.* Dogs Throughout History. New York: PowerKids Press, 2000.

Schopell, M. William. *Guide to Owning a Dachshund.* Popular Dog Library. Philadelphia: Chelsea House Publishers, 1999.

You can read articles about Dachshunds in *AKC Gazette, Dog and Kennel, Dog Fancy, Dogs in Canada,* and *Dog World.*

Useful Addresses

American Kennel Club
5580 Centerview Drive
Raleigh, NC 27606

Canadian Kennel Club
89 Skyway Avenue
Suite 100
Etobicoke, ON M9W 6R4
Canada

Dachshund Club of America
1793 Berme Road
Kerhonkson, NY 12446

Miniature Dachshund Club of Canada
255 Pine Grove Road
Woodbridge, ON L4L 2H7
Canada

National Miniature Dachshund Club
31030 108th Street
Princeton, MN 55371-4646

Internet Sites

American Kennel Club
http://www.akc.org

Canadian Kennel Club
http://www.ckc.ca

Dachshund Club of America
http://www.dachshund-dca.org

Dachsies
http://www.dachsie.org

Wiener Dogs
htpp://www.wienerdogs.org/mainpage.html

Index